ED EMBERLEY'S

A B C

LITTLE, BROWN AND COMPANY
BOSTON —TORONTO

FIRST EDITION *
T 04/78

LIBRARY OF CONGRESS
CATALOGING IN PUBLICATION DATA

EMBERLEY, ED.
  ED EMBERLEY'S ABC
  SUMMARY: ANIMALS ENGAGING IN A
VARIETY OF ACTIVITIES INTRODUCE
THE LETTERS OF THE ALPHABET.
  [1. ALPHABET BOOKS] I. TITLE. II. TITLE: ABC.

    PZ7.E565Aad   [E]   77-28099
    ISBN 0-316-23408-7

PUBLISHED SIMULTANEOUSLY
IN CANADA BY
LITTLE, BROWN AND COMPANY
(CANADA) LIMITED.

PRINTED IN THE UNITED STATES OF AMERICA

ANT

BEAR

CROW

DOGS

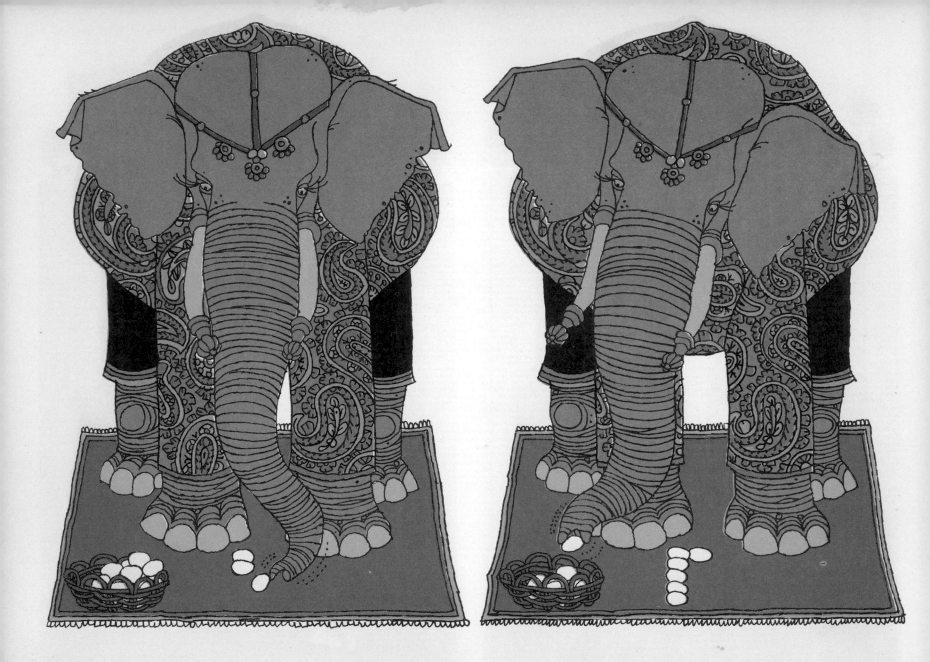

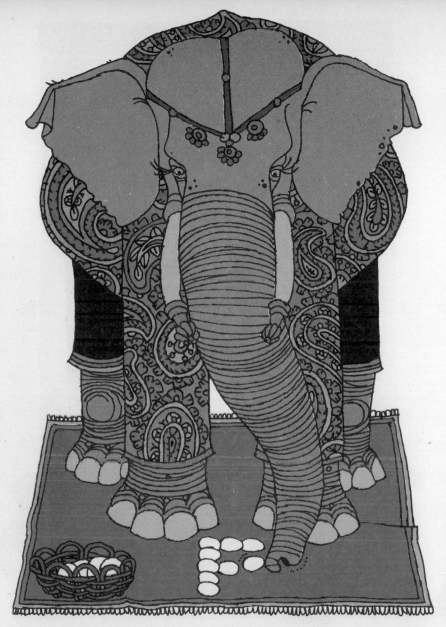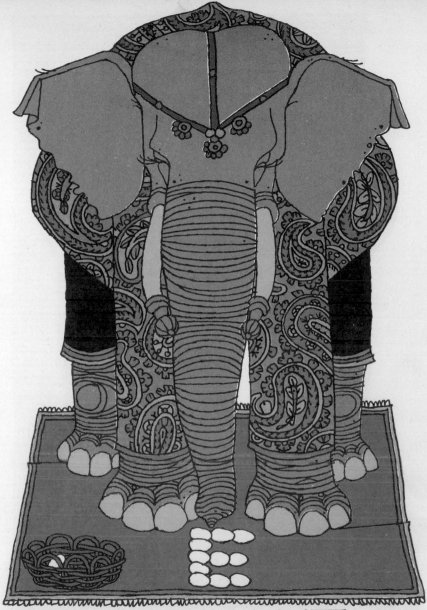

ELEPHANT

FROGS

GEESE

HEN

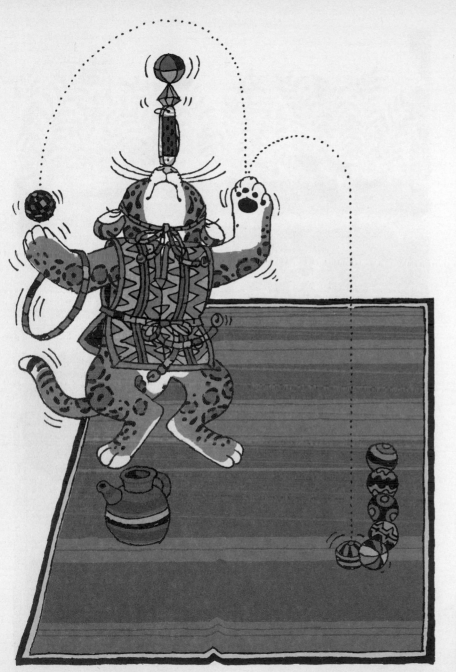
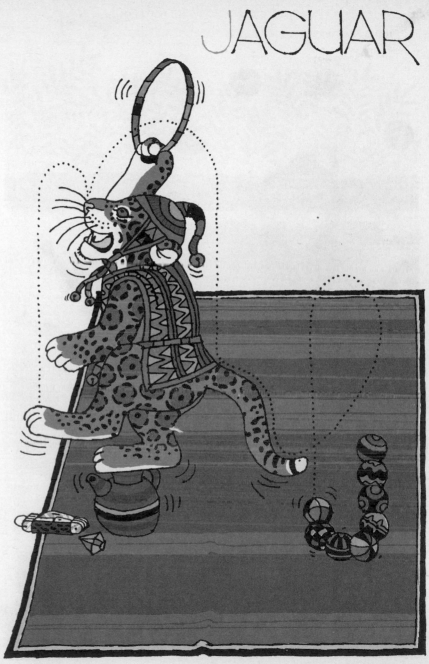

KIWI

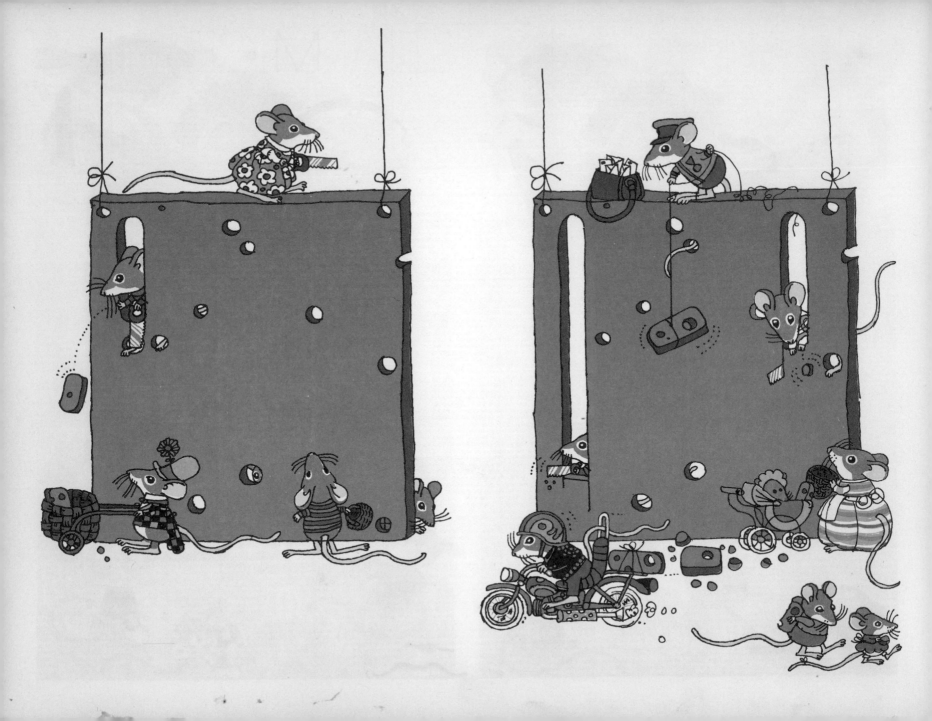

MICE

LION

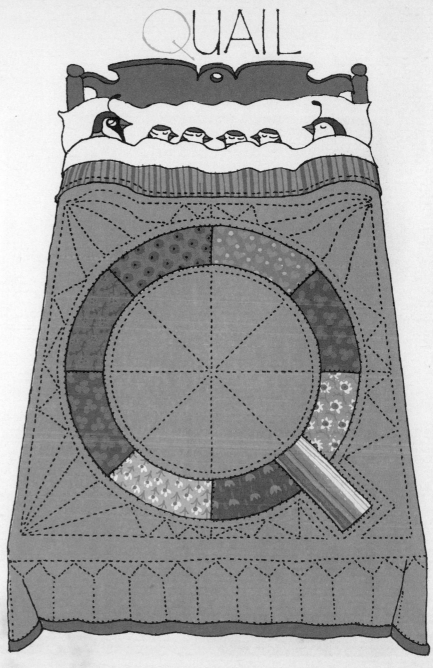

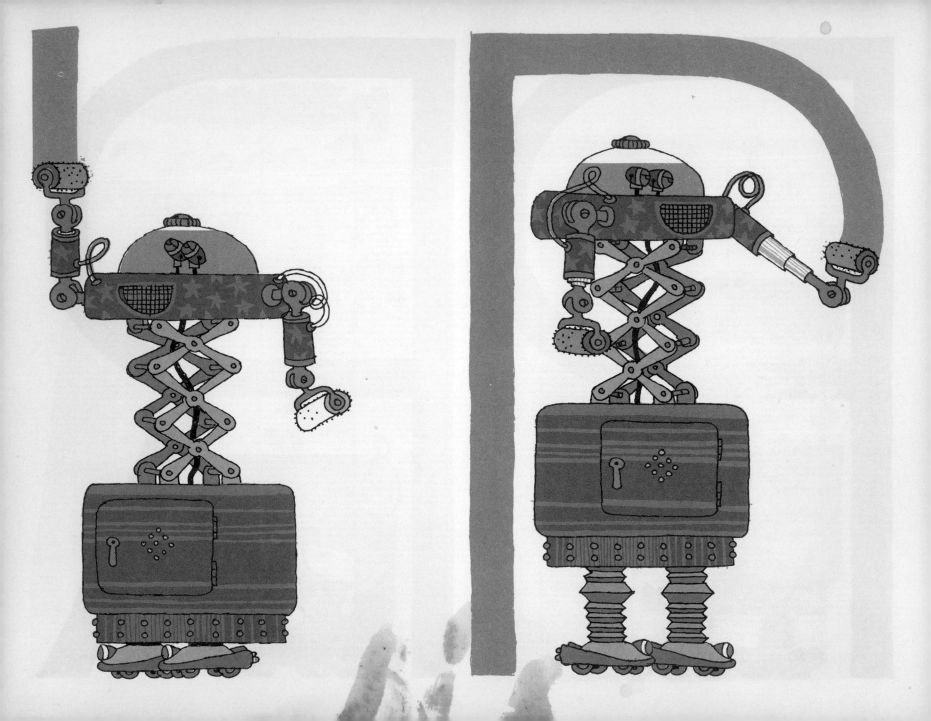

RABBIT

SNAILS

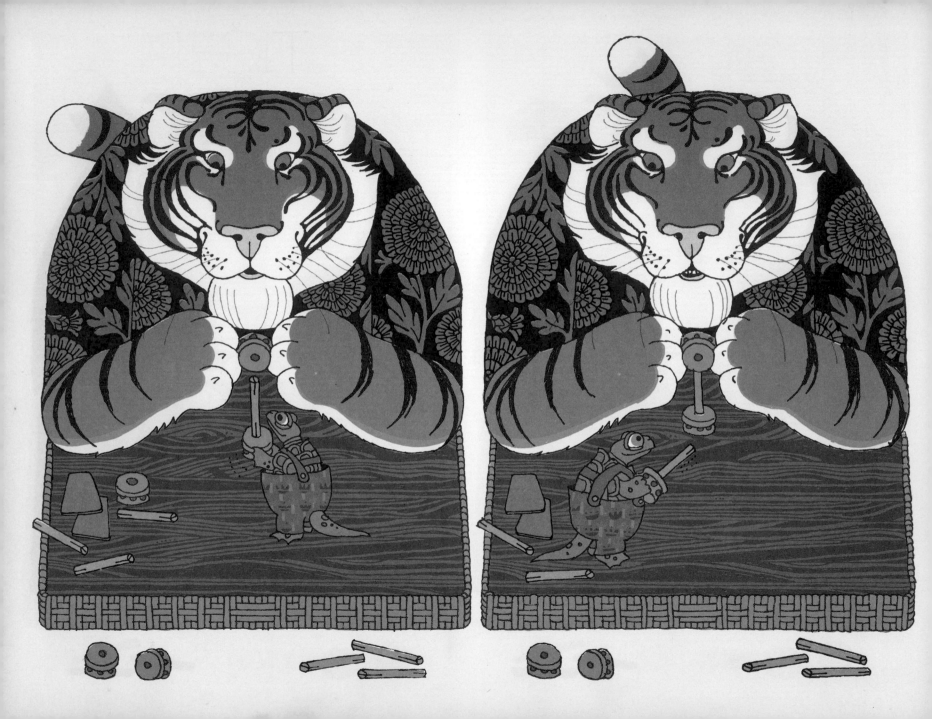

UNICORN

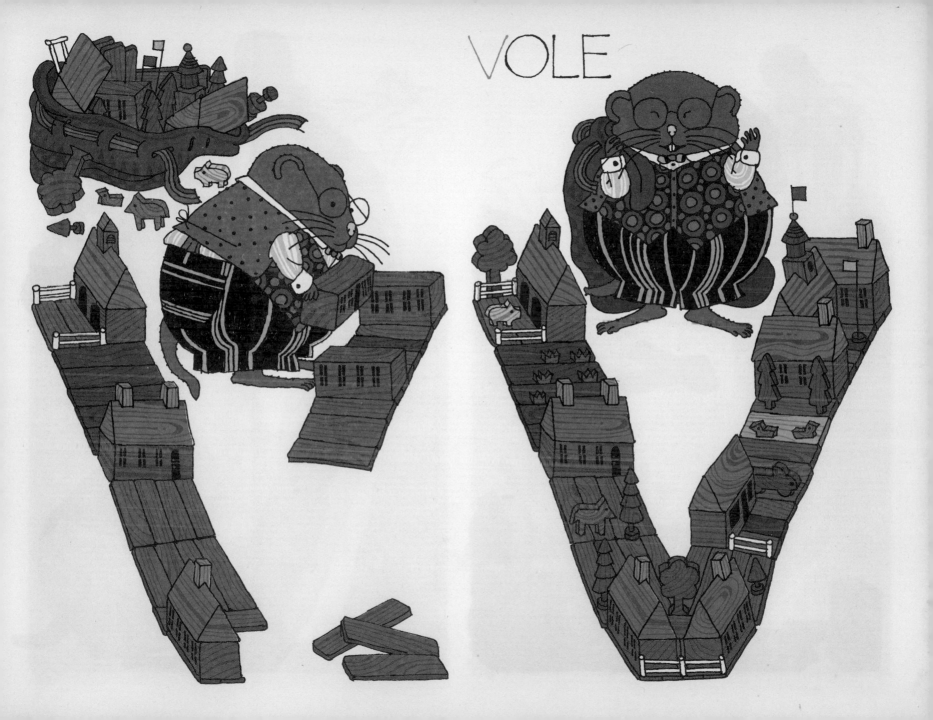

VOLE

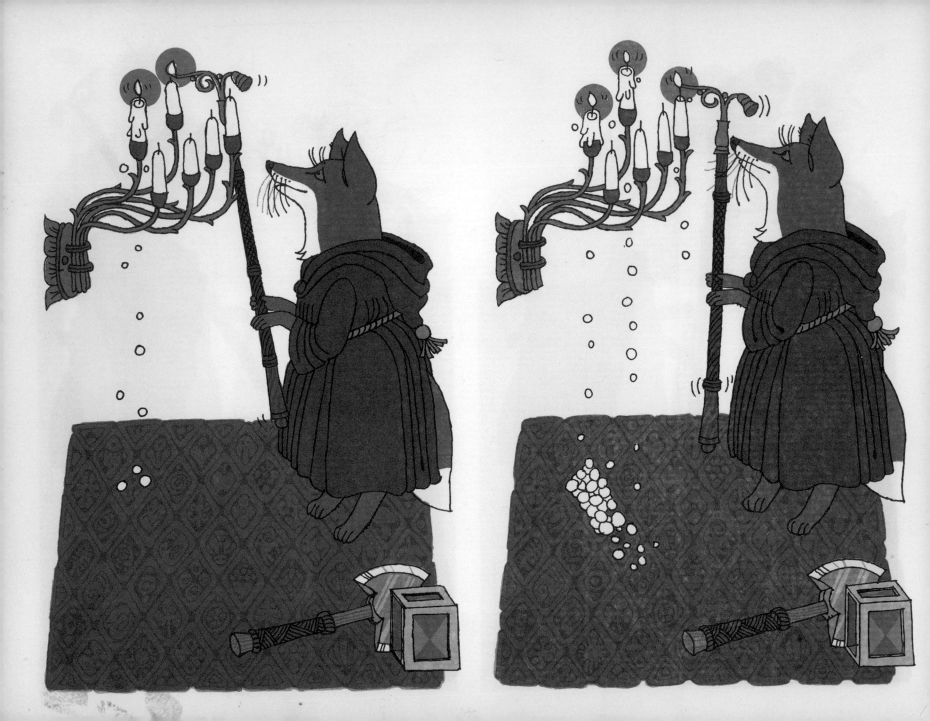

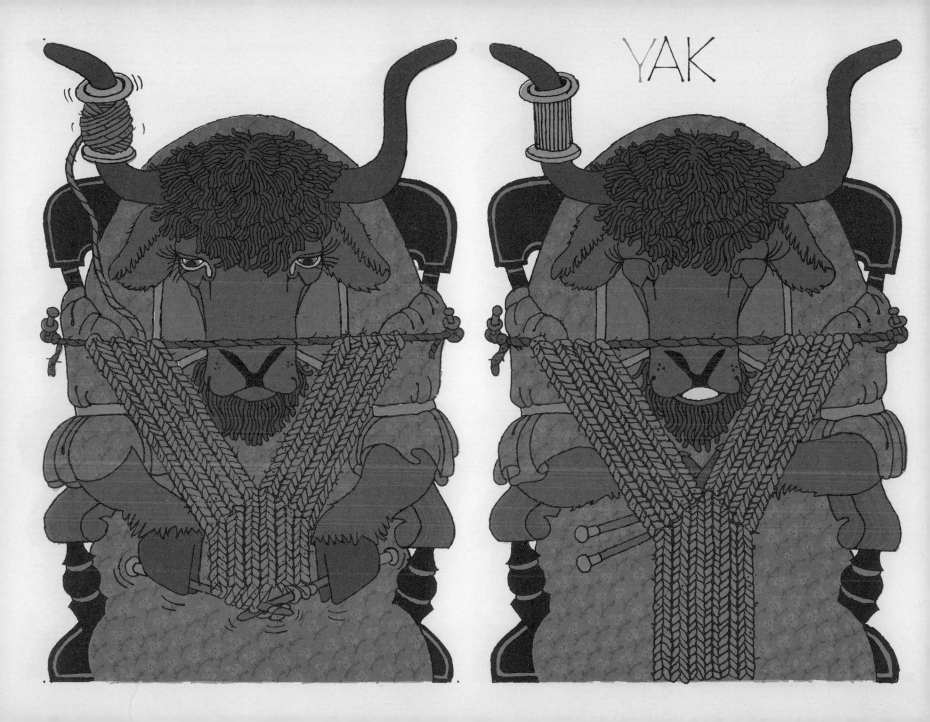

YAK

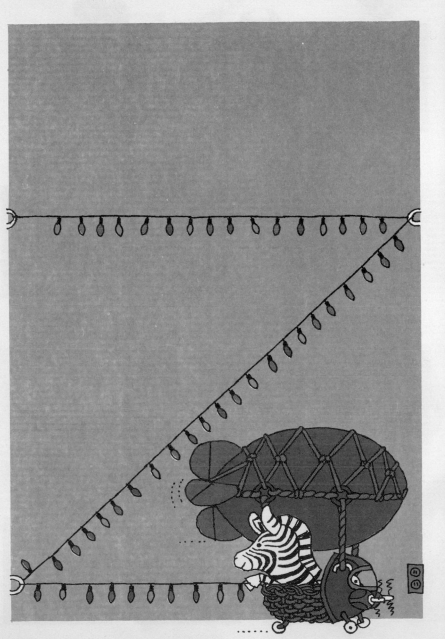
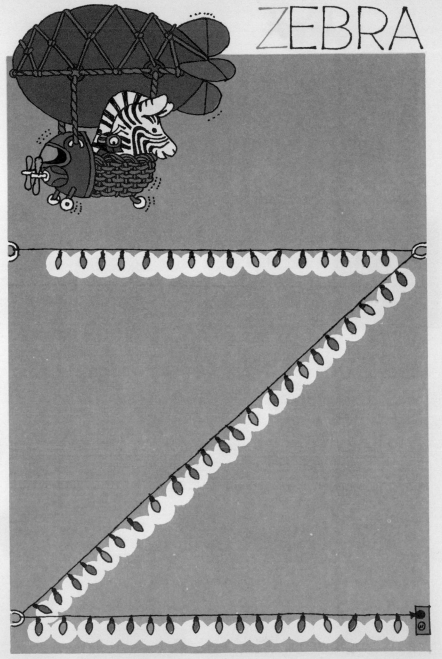

SOME THINGS FOR YOU TO FIND.

A ANT, ALLIGATOR, AIRPLANE.
B BEAR, BAMBOO BASKET, BUG, BIRD,
  BLUE, BROWN, BLACK, BERRIES.
C CROW CRICKET, CORN, CLOWN.
D DOG, DIGGING, DINOSAUR (BONES)
  DAISEY, DUMP TRUCK.
E ELEPHANT, EGGS, ELEVEN.
F FROG, FIRE FLIES, FLOWERS, FIDDLE,
  FIVE, FOUR.
G GOOSE, GANDER, GOSLING, GEESE,
  GOLF, GRASS, GRASSHOPPER,
  GREEN, GRAY, GRAPES, GERANIUMS
H HORSE, HEN HAY, HOOF, HELPING.
★ I PIG, PIN, PINK, RIBBON.
J JAGUAR, JUG, JUGGLER,
  JEWEL, JACKNIFE.
K KIWI, KOALA, KANGAROO.
L LIZARD, LOBSTER, LINE, LITTLE.
M MICE, MOUSE, MOTHER, MAIL.
★ N LION, RACOON, RIBBON, LEMON, GREEN,
  BROWN, FAN, MOON, CAN, SPOON,
O OWL, ORANGE, ORANGUTAN.
P PARROT, PIRATE, PINK, PURPLE, PAINT,
  PUFFIN, PAIR, PARAKEETS.
Q QUAIL, QUILT.
R RABBIT, ROBOT, RED, ROLLER.

S SNAIL, SINGING, SILENT, SIX,
  SEVEN, SUBMARINE, SALAMANDER,
  SAILOR, STRING, STONES.
T TIGER, TURTLE, TRAY.
★ U UNICORN, UNICYCLE, UMBRELLA,
  2 UKELELE (ONE YELLOW, ONE BLACK)
  UNGUICULATE
V VOLE, VILLAGE, VEST, VEGETABLES,
W WALRUS, WATERFALL,
  WILLOW, WOODPECKER.
★ X FOX, BOX, AX WAX SIX
Y YAK, YELLOW, YARN.
Z ZEBRA, ZEPPLIN.

BARBARA AND ED EMBERLEY, THEIR MARK

ART WORK FINISHED, CAMERA READY
JANUARY 18, 1978
BLACK LINE DRAWINGS BY ED EMBERLEY.
COLOR OVERLAYS BY BARBARA EMBERLEY,
COLOR OVERLAYS FOR BEAR AND RABBIT
PAGES BY MICHAEL EMBERLEY.